Unshakable
FAITH

An Inspirational Growth Book

Biblion Publishing LLC.

Unshakable
FAITH

An Inspirational Growth Book

Biblion
Publishing LLC.

Unshakable Faith

First Edition / First Printing

Getting the most out of the
Unshakable Faith book

Are you ready to grow your faith like never before? Do you want to walk in the favor of faith that God has planned for you? Do you need a daily guide and reading plan to get you to a new place of your faith? If you answered yes to any of these questions, this book is for you! "Unshakable Faith" will take you on a journey to realize the blessings that God has ordained for you to walk in right now! Each day presents a personal quote along with a plan of action and reflections for each reading. Unshakable Faith will help you reach a. new level of faith! You will learn new ways to stay motivated and inspired. You will walk in a newness of joy, peace, contentment, abundance and prosperity as you complete each daily guide and reading plan in this book. Get ready to be blessed beyond what you can think or imagine, as you begin to possess a new a level of faith that is unshakable!

Dedication

To my Daddy, Anthony T. Pleasant, who was a perfect example to me of a real man. To my wife Kimberly, whom I love dearly. To my children; Christian, Zion, and Nacara.

To my New Zion Christian Church Family and Clark Atlanta University, thanks for allowing me to be used by God to bless others!

Humbly Yours in Christ,

Apostle Jamie T. Pleasant

"Unshakable Faith"
Growth book synopsis

Congratulations on purchasing this book! Get ready to achieve a new level of faith through your daily reading through this growth book. This book is filled with inspirational quotes that God Yahweh personally spoke to me to share with you. This book will guide you into a deeper revelation of God's plan for increasing your faith to live a triumphant life, beginning now!

²³ Buy truth, and do not sell it;
buy wisdom, instruction, and understanding.

Proverbs 23:23 (ESV)

This
UnShakable Faith

Growth Book
belongs to:

_____

_____

_____

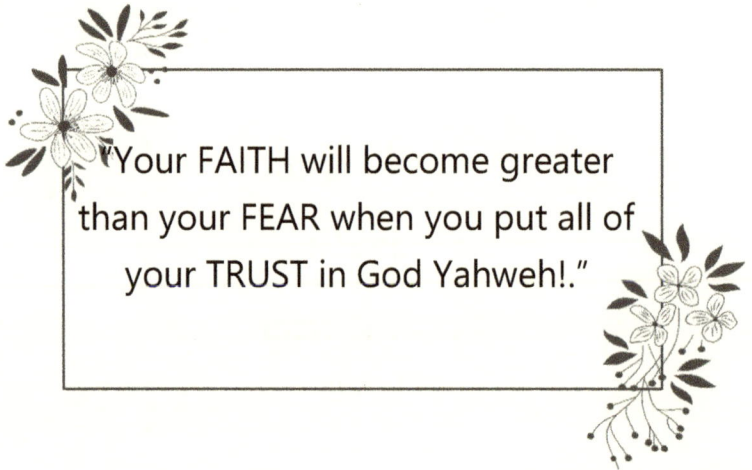

"Your FAITH will become greater
than your FEAR when you put all of
your TRUST in God Yahweh!."

What This Means to Me

My Action Plan

_____

_____

_____

_____

_____

_____

_____

Personal Blessings I Have Experienced

Personal Reflection and Final Thoughts

"Faith only works, when you do."

What This Means to Me

My Action Plan

_____

_____

_____

_____

_____

_____

Personal Blessings I Have Experienced

Personal Reflection and Final Thoughts

"The same way DOUBT creates mountains, FAITH can remove them!".

What This Means to Me

My Action Plan

_____

_____

_____

_____

_____

_____

_____

Personal Blessings I Have Experienced

Personal Reflection and Final Thoughts

_____

_____

_____

_____

_____

_____

_____

_____

_____

_____

_____

_____

_____

_____

_____

_____

_____

_____

_____

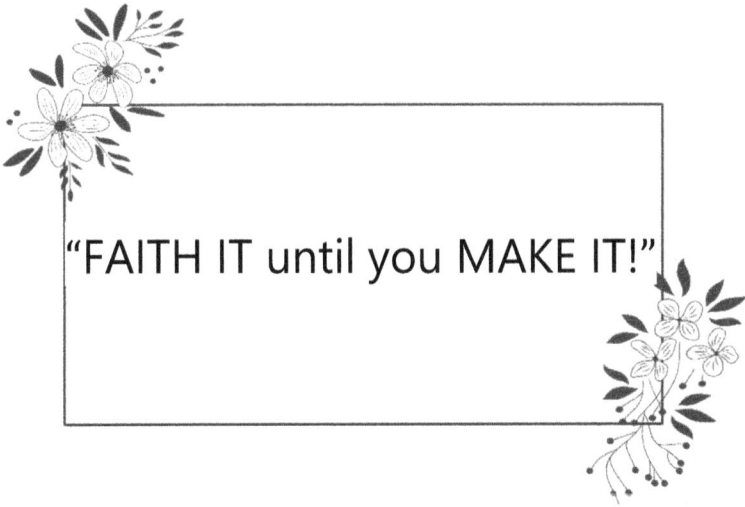

"FAITH IT until you MAKE IT!"

What This Means to Me

My Action Plan

Personal Blessings I Have Experienced

Personal Reflection and Final Thoughts

_____

_____

_____

_____

_____

_____

_____

_____

_____

_____

_____

_____

_____

_____

_____

_____

_____

_____

"Faith is the foundation of favor that lasts forever!."

What This Means to Me

My Action Plan

Personal Blessings I Have Experienced

Personal Reflection and Final Thoughts

"I promise not to force my FAITH on you if you promise not to force your FEAR on me."

What This Means to Me

My Action Plan

Personal Blessings I Have Experienced

Personal Reflection and Final Thoughts

_____

_____

_____

_____

_____

_____

_____

_____

_____

_____

_____

_____

_____

_____

_____

_____

_____

_____

"Faith without works produces spiritual unemployment."

What This Means to Me

My Action Plan

_____

_____

_____

_____

_____

_____

_____

Personal Blessings I Have Experienced

Personal Reflection and Final Thoughts

"FEED your FAITH and FEAR will FLEE!"

What This Means to Me

My Action Plan

Personal Blessings I Have Experienced

Personal Reflection and Final Thoughts

"Without faith, you will be without."

What This Means to Me

My Action Plan

Personal Blessings I Have Experienced

Personal Reflection and Final Thoughts

_____

_____

_____

_____

_____

_____

_____

_____

_____

_____

_____

_____

_____

_____

_____

_____

_____

_____

"Faith that is the size of a grain of a mustard seed, will produce fruit the size of a mountain."

What This Means to Me

My Action Plan

_____

_____

_____

_____

_____

_____

Personal Blessings I Have Experienced

Personal Reflection and Final Thoughts

"Faith doesn't make sense; it makes things happen."

What This Means to Me

My Action Plan

Personal Blessings I Have Experienced

Personal Reflection and Final Thoughts

_____
_____
_____
_____
_____
_____
_____
_____
_____
_____
_____
_____
_____
_____
_____
_____
_____
_____
_____
_____

"Faith comes by HEARING
and DOING."

What This Means to Me

My Action Plan

_____

_____

_____

_____

_____

_____

Personal Blessings I Have Experienced

Personal Reflection and Final Thoughts

"You can either WALK by FAITH or RUN in FEAR."

What This Means to Me

My Action Plan

Personal Blessings I Have Experienced

Personal Reflection and Final Thoughts

_____

_____

_____

_____

_____

_____

_____

_____

_____

_____

_____

_____

_____

_____

_____

_____

_____

_____

"Faith is the Title Deed that is based on spiritual SEED."

What This Means to Me

My Action Plan

Personal Blessings I Have Experienced

Personal Reflection and Final Thoughts

"Faith SEES, what the EYES can't. "

What This Means to Me

My Action Plan

Personal Blessings I Have Experienced

Personal Reflection and Final Thoughts

_____

_____

_____

_____

_____

_____

_____

_____

_____

_____

_____

_____

_____

_____

_____

_____

_____

_____

_____

_____

_____

"Without FAITH, it's
IMPOSSIBLE to see the
POSSIBLE."

What This Means to Me

My Action Plan

Personal Blessings I Have Experienced

Personal Reflection and Final Thoughts

"Faith HEALS, where it HURTS."

What This Means to Me

My Action Plan

_____

_____

_____

_____

_____

_____

_____

Personal Blessings I Have Experienced

Personal Reflection and Final Thoughts

_____

_____

_____

_____

_____

_____

_____

_____

_____

_____

_____

_____

_____

_____

_____

_____

_____

_____

_____

"Faith will write a check that your life must cash."

What This Means to Me

My Action Plan

Personal Blessings I Have Experienced

Personal Reflection and Final Thoughts

"Faith can raise the DEAD
and the LIVING."

What This Means to Me

My Action Plan

Personal Blessings I Have Experienced

Personal Reflection and Final Thoughts

_____

_____

_____

_____

_____

_____

_____

_____

_____

_____

_____

_____

_____

_____

_____

_____

_____

"There is no greater display of faith, than to become less worried."

What This Means to Me

My Action Plan

Personal Blessings I Have Experienced

Personal Reflection and Final Thoughts

"Your faith will be credited as righteousness when you charge it to God."

What This Means to Me

My Action Plan

Personal Blessings I Have Experienced

Personal Reflection and Final Thoughts

_____
_____
_____
_____
_____
_____
_____
_____
_____
_____
_____
_____
_____
_____
_____
_____
_____
_____
_____
_____
_____
_____

"Faith is, declaring, what you desire."

What This Means to Me

My Action Plan

Personal Blessings I Have Experienced

Personal Reflection and Final Thoughts

"Faith will transform your
HATERS into
APPRECIATERS."

What This Means to Me

My Action Plan

Personal Blessings I Have Experienced

Personal Reflection and Final Thoughts

"Faith HEALS, when life HURTS!"

What This Means to Me

My Action Plan

Personal Blessings I Have Experienced

Personal Reflection and Final Thoughts

_____

_____

_____

_____

_____

_____

_____

_____

_____

_____

_____

_____

_____

_____

_____

_____

_____

_____

"Faith will transform you into someone you thought you could never be."

What This Means to Me

My Action Plan

Personal Blessings I Have Experienced

Personal Reflection and Final Thoughts

"You will see an increase in faith, when you increase your purpose."

What This Means to Me

My Action Plan

_____

_____

_____

_____

_____

_____

Personal Blessings I Have Experienced

Personal Reflection and Final Thoughts

_____

_____

_____

_____

_____

_____

_____

_____

_____

_____

_____

_____

_____

_____

_____

_____

_____

_____

"The object of your faith, should always be to please God Yahweh."

What This Means to Me

My Action Plan

Personal Blessings I Have Experienced

Personal Reflection and Final Thoughts

_____

_____

_____

_____

_____

_____

_____

_____

_____

_____

_____

_____

_____

_____

_____

_____

_____

_____

_____

"The author of your faith, is
the writer of your life."

What This Means to Me

My Action Plan

Personal Blessings I Have Experienced

Personal Reflection and Final Thoughts

"Now faith, brings future blessings!"

What This Means to Me

My Action Plan

_____

_____

_____

_____

_____

_____

_____

Personal Blessings I Have Experienced

Personal Reflection and Final Thoughts

"The author of your faith is the fixer of your fear."

What This Means to Me

My Action Plan

Personal Blessings I Have Experienced

Personal Reflection and Final Thoughts

_____

_____

_____

_____

_____

_____

_____

_____

_____

_____

_____

_____

_____

_____

_____

_____

_____

_____

_____

"Faith answers, what others question."

What This Means to Me

My Action Plan

Personal Blessings I Have Experienced

Personal Reflection and Final Thoughts

_____

_____

_____

_____

_____

_____

_____

_____

_____

_____

_____

_____

_____

_____

_____

_____

_____

"Stop trying to FIT in, when you were born to STAND out!"

What This Means to Me

My Action Plan

Personal Blessings I Have Experienced

Personal Reflection and Final Thoughts

"God Yahweh did not create us to WANT. He created us to WILL!"

What This Means to Me

My Action Plan

_____

_____

_____

_____

_____

_____

Personal Blessings I Have Experienced

Personal Reflection and Final Thoughts

"When you learn how to SEE the INVISIBLE, you will be able to do the IMPOSSIBLE!"

What This Means to Me

My Action Plan

Personal Blessings I Have Experienced

Personal Reflection and Final Thoughts

"The MORE you THANK God Yahweh for what you have, the more He'll GIVE you to be THANKFUL for!"

What This Means to Me

My Action Plan

Personal Blessings I Have Experienced

Personal Reflection and Final Thoughts

_____

_____

_____

_____

_____

_____

_____

_____

_____

_____

_____

_____

_____

_____

_____

_____

_____

_____

"FAILURE is not the opposite of SUCCESS. It is a part of the PROCESS of SUCCESS!"

What This Means to Me

My Action Plan

Personal Blessings I Have Experienced

Personal Reflection and Final Thoughts

"Don't be afraid to TRY. Be afraid, NOT to!"

What This Means to Me

My Action Plan

Personal Blessings I Have Experienced

Personal Reflection and Final Thoughts

"There are TWO types of people who will tell you that you won't MAKE IT in life: Those who are AFRAID to try and those who are afraid you will SUCCEED."

What This Means to Me

My Action Plan

Personal Blessings I Have Experienced

Personal Reflection and Final Thoughts

"The FASTEST way to kill a BIG DREAM, is to tell it to a SMALL MINDED person."

What This Means to Me

My Action Plan

Personal Blessings I Have Experienced

Personal Reflection and Final Thoughts

"CURSED people, CURSE people. BLESSED people, BLESS people."

What This Means to Me

My Action Plan

_____

_____

_____

_____

_____

_____

_____

Personal Blessings I Have Experienced

Personal Reflection and Final Thoughts

"This is the season where what was HARD for you to REACH, will now REACH out to you!"

What This Means to Me

My Action Plan

Personal Blessings I Have Experienced

Personal Reflection and Final Thoughts

_____

_____

_____

_____

_____

_____

_____

_____

_____

_____

_____

_____

_____

_____

_____

_____

_____

_____

_____

_____

"God's UNCHANGING hand
will CHANGE you!"

What This Means to Me

My Action Plan

Personal Blessings I Have Experienced

Personal Reflection and Final Thoughts

"If you don't learn how to become PATIENT, you will end up being one."

What This Means to Me

My Action Plan

Personal Blessings I Have Experienced

Personal Reflection and Final Thoughts

_____

_____

_____

_____

_____

_____

_____

_____

_____

_____

_____

_____

_____

_____

_____

_____

_____

_____

_____

_____

"ENVY always HATES the level of EXCELLENCE it can not REACH!"

What This Means to Me

My Action Plan

Personal Blessings I Have Experienced

Personal Reflection and Final Thoughts

_____

_____

_____

_____

_____

_____

_____

_____

_____

_____

_____

_____

_____

_____

_____

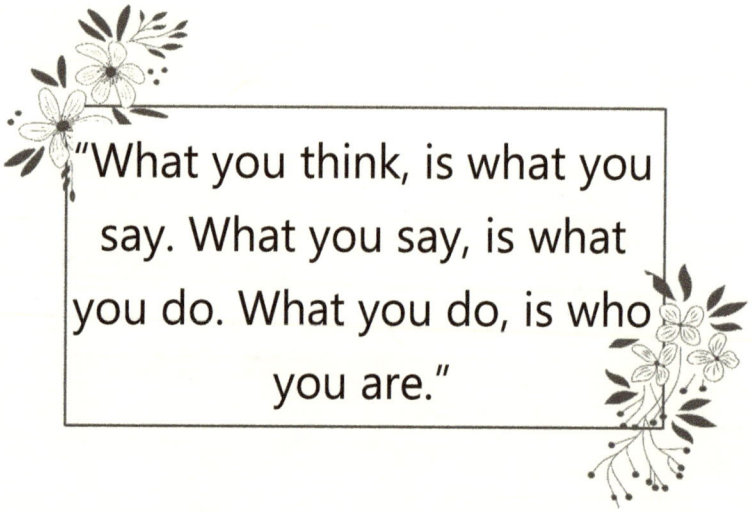

"What you think, is what you say. What you say, is what you do. What you do, is who you are."

What This Means to Me

My Action Plan

Personal Blessings I Have Experienced

Personal Reflection and Final Thoughts

_____

_____

_____

_____

_____

_____

_____

_____

_____

_____

_____

_____

_____

_____

_____

_____

_____

_____

"Make your HATERS your ELEVATORS!"

What This Means to Me

My Action Plan

Personal Blessings I Have Experienced

Personal Reflection and Final Thoughts

"You can't be ANYTHING to ANYONE, until you are EVERYTHING to YOURSELF!"

What This Means to Me

My Action Plan

Personal Blessings I Have Experienced

Personal Reflection and Final Thoughts

_____

_____

_____

_____

_____

_____

_____

_____

_____

_____

_____

_____

_____

_____

_____

_____

"The more time you spend with God Yahweh, the more, He will spend on you!"

What This Means to Me

My Action Plan

Personal Blessings I Have Experienced

Personal Reflection and Final Thoughts

"When you KNEEL before God, you can STAND before men!"

What This Means to Me

My Action Plan

Personal Blessings I Have Experienced

Personal Reflection and Final Thoughts

"JEALOUSY always hates
what it can't become!"

What This Means to Me

My Action Plan

Personal Blessings I Have Experienced

Personal Reflection and Final Thoughts

"If you want MORE, you have to go where MORE is!"

What This Means to Me

My Action Plan

Personal Blessings I Have Experienced

Personal Reflection and Final Thoughts

"PATIENCE is a VIRTUE, and it carries a LOT of WAIT!"

What This Means to Me

My Action Plan

Personal Blessings I Have Experienced

Personal Reflection and Final Thoughts

"Never sell yourself short! Reach above your comfort zone. That's where your next blessing is!"

What This Means to Me

My Action Plan

Personal Blessings I Have Experienced

Personal Reflection and Final Thoughts

"You can't share your BIG dreams with people that have SMALL minds!"

What This Means to Me

My Action Plan

Personal Blessings I Have Experienced

Personal Reflection and Final Thoughts

"When you SETTLE, you become UNSETTLED!"

What This Means to Me

My Action Plan

Personal Blessings I Have Experienced

Personal Reflection and Final Thoughts

_____

_____

_____

_____

_____

_____

_____

_____

_____

_____

_____

_____

_____

_____

_____

_____

_____

_____

_____

_____

"No one can make you feel INFERIOR without your CONSENT!"

What This Means to Me

My Action Plan

_____

_____

_____

_____

_____

_____

_____

Personal Blessings I Have Experienced

Personal Reflection and Final Thoughts

"The first step to GOING where you have never been, is to decide you are not going to STAY there!"

What This Means to Me

My Action Plan

Personal Blessings I Have Experienced

Personal Reflection and Final Thoughts

"Never, ever, measure your success by someone else's ruler!"

What This Means to Me

My Action Plan

Personal Blessings I Have Experienced

Personal Reflection and Final Thoughts

"Success is missed by most people
because it is dressed in hard work
and perseverance."

What This Means to Me

My Action Plan

_____

_____

_____

_____

_____

_____

_____

Personal Blessings I Have Experienced

Personal Reflection and Final Thoughts

"A real friend is someone who RUNS in for you, when everyone else WALKS out on you."

What This Means to Me

My Action Plan

_____

_____

_____

_____

_____

_____

Personal Blessings I Have Experienced

Personal Reflection and Final Thoughts

"You should never LOSE at anything! You should either WIN or GROW from it!"

What This Means to Me

My Action Plan

_____

_____

_____

_____

_____

_____

_____

Personal Blessings I Have Experienced

Personal Reflection and Final Thoughts

"The fruit of faith comes from a Godly word sown in season."

What This Means to Me

My Action Plan

Personal Blessings I Have Experienced

Personal Reflection and Final Thoughts

_____

_____

_____

_____

_____

_____

_____

_____

_____

_____

_____

_____

_____

_____

_____

_____

"Faith always says, I CAN DO IT!"

What This Means to Me

My Action Plan

_____

_____

_____

_____

_____

_____

Personal Blessings I Have Experienced

Personal Reflection and Final Thoughts

_____

_____

_____

_____

_____

_____

_____

_____

_____

_____

_____

_____

_____

_____

_____

_____

_____

_____

"Don't just GO through it,
GROW through it!"

What This Means to Me

My Action Plan

Personal Blessings I Have Experienced

Personal Reflection and Final Thoughts

"UNQUALIFIED people aren't QUALIFIED to QUALIFY you!"

What This Means to Me

My Action Plan

_____

_____

_____

_____

_____

_____

_____

Personal Blessings I Have Experienced

Personal Reflection and Final Thoughts

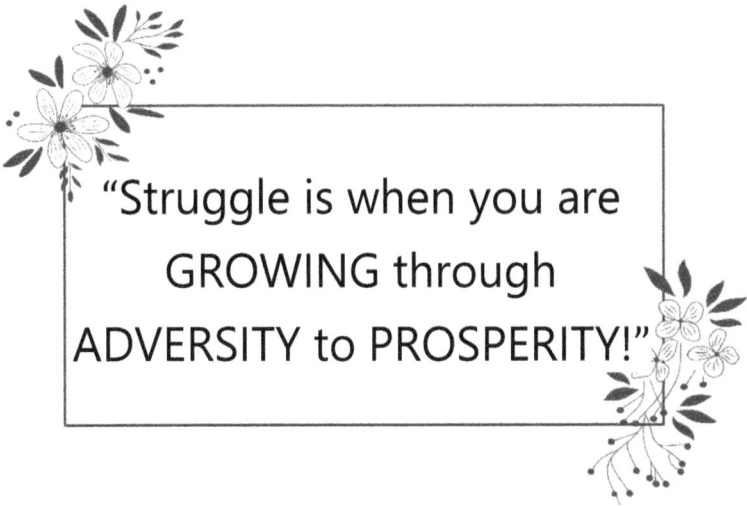

"Struggle is when you are GROWING through ADVERSITY to PROSPERITY!"

What This Means to Me

My Action Plan

Personal Blessings I Have Experienced

Personal Reflection and Final Thoughts

"Don't ever let anyone DULL your SHINE!"

What This Means to Me

My Action Plan

Personal Blessings I Have Experienced

Personal Reflection and Final Thoughts

_____

_____

_____

_____

_____

_____

_____

_____

_____

_____

_____

_____

_____

_____

_____

_____

_____

_____

_____

_____

"PEOPLE have a right to their OPINION of you, and you have a RIGHT to IGNORE Them!"

What This Means to Me

My Action Plan

Personal Blessings I Have Experienced

Personal Reflection and Final Thoughts

_____

_____

_____

_____

_____

_____

_____

_____

_____

_____

_____

_____

_____

_____

_____

_____

"WEALTH is not a measure of
how MUCH you MAKE, but
how MUCH you KEEP!"

What This Means to Me

My Action Plan

_____

_____

_____

_____

_____

_____

_____

Personal Blessings I Have Experienced

Personal Reflection and Final Thoughts

Epilogue

One of the best ways to experience God's prosperity in your life is for you to give your life to Christ Jesus. Repeat these simple words and it will be a done deal. Repeat the following: Lord Christ Jesus as of this very moment, I accept you as Lord and Savior of my life. I now give my life to you to be fashioned for your purpose and glory. Lord, all of these things that I have said, I truly believe in my heart and have confessed with my mouth to you. I know now that I have received everlasting life based on the work that Christ has done and will continue to do in my life. Lord Christ, thank you for bringing me to this point of my life where I surrender my all to you. It is in the Holy Spirit through Christ Jesus, I say Amen.

Humbly Yours in Christ

Apostle Jamie T. Pleasant

Book Dr. Jamie Pleasant for a Speaking Engagement!

For speaking engagements, please contact Dr. Jamie T. Pleasant at admin@newzionchristianchurch.org or 678.845.7055

About the Author

Apostle Jamie T. Pleasant, Ph.D., a modern-day polymath, is the founder and Chief Executive Pastor of New Zion Christian Church in Suwanee, Georgia. He currently serves as the Dean of Graduate Education at Clark Atlanta University. He is also a tenured Full Professor of Marketing at Clark Atlanta University's School of Business. Notably, he is the first faculty member in the university's history to be accepted into Mensa International, the world's largest and oldest high IQ society for individuals who have scored in the 98th percentile or above on an intelligence test.

Dr. Pleasant is the first African American to graduate from the Georgia Institute of Technology (Georgia Tech) with a Ph.D. in Business Management with a concentration in Marketing, earning that degree in August 1999. He is a 2016 recipient of the "Lifetime Achievement Award" from former President Barack Obama for volunteer and community service. He was awarded the "Game Changer" Educator Award by Reverend Jesse Jackson at the 2019 Rainbow PUSH International Convention. As a polyhistor, in addition to obtaining a doctorate degree in Business Management from the Georgia Institute of Technology, he holds a bachelor's degree in Physics from Benedict College in Columbia, South Carolina, Marketing Studies from Clemson University and an M.B.A. in Marketing from the very prestigious, Clark Atlanta University.

Under his leadership, New Zion has grown from three members when it started in 1995 to well over 700 in weekly attendance, with a focus on economic and entrepreneurial development. God gave him the vision to establish a Biblically based economic development initiative for New Zion Christian Church. He remains at the pulse of the economic business sector.

As a result, Apostle Pleasant is in constant demand to train, speak and teach others at all levels in ministry and the private sector about business and economic development across the country. He has created numerous cutting edge and industry leading ministerial, business and economic development classes and programs, along with SAT & PSAT prep courses for children ages 9-19. He founded The Financial Literacy Academy for Youth (FLAFY), where youth between the ages of 13-19 attend 12-week intense classes on financial money management principles. At the end of those 12 weeks, they receive a "Personal Finance" certificate of achievement. In 2015, he established The Young Leadership and Success Academy that teaches young people between the ages of 10-21 how to invest, make presentations and start and operate businesses. Other ministries he has pioneered include The Wealth Builders Investment Club (WBIC), which educates and allows members to actively invest in the stock market, along with the much-celebrated Institute of Entrepreneurship (IOE), where participants earn a certificate in entrepreneurship after three months of comprehensive training in all aspects of starting and owning a successful competitive business. The main goal and purpose of IOE is that each year one of the trained businesses will be awarded up to $10,000 startup money to ensure financial success.

Apostle Pleasant has met with political officials such as former President Bill Clinton and Nelson Mandela. He has performed marriage ceremonies and counseled numerous celebrated personalities such as Usher Raymond, Terri Vaughn, and many others. Several gospel music artists have performed at the church, including Tiff Joy. Each year, Apostle Pleasant conducts chapel services for Clemson University's football team and is a spiritual and personal friend to its two-time national championship head coach, Dabo Swinney.

As a modern-day civil rights leader, he is a close aide to Reverend Jesse Jackson and serves on the Board of Directors of Rainbow PUSH Inc. (Atlanta) and Director of Business Education and Corporate Engagement. He serves on the Board of Fellowship of Christian Athletes (Atlanta Urban) and after the Columbine High School shooting, he founded the National School Safety Advocacy Association. His latest foundations include the Young Entrepreneurship Program (YEP) and the African American Consumer Economic Rights (AACER).

He has authored numerous books that include: *Powerful Prayers That Open Heaven, Capturing and Keeping the Pastor's Heart, Advertising Principles: How to Effectively Reach African Americans in the 21ˢᵗ Century, Discover a New You: A 21 Day Journey to Uncovering Your Uniqueness, Daily Quotes for Daily*

Blessings, The Making of a Man, I'm Just Sayin', From My Heart To Yours: Love Letters From A Loving Father, Today's Apostle: Servants of God Leading His People towards Unity, A 7 Day Prayer Plan for Prosperity, You Have What It Takes, A Marketing Model for Ethnic Consumer Behavior, An Overview of Strategic Healthcare Marketing and The Importance of Subcultural Marketing.

Apostle Pleasant is a lifetime member of Alpha Phi Alpha Fraternity Inc. He is the loving husband of the pulchritudinous Kimberly Pleasant and the proud father of three children: Christian, Zion and Nacara.

FINI

www.ingramcontent.com/pod-product-compliance
Lightning Source LLC
Chambersburg PA
CBHW020511100426
42813CB00030B/3193/J